LIFE CLASS

Jo Reed was born near Durham in 1941. She spent her childhood moving up and down the East Coast, from Northumbria to Norfolk, before arriving in Soho, London in the 1960s. She later lived in rural Surrey and Lincolnshire, before settling in Scarborough, North Yorkshire, at the turn of the century.

She has worked as an illustrator, printmaker and teacher, and recently completed an MA in Creative Writing from Newcastle University. Her debut collection of poetry, *Stone Venus*, was published by Valley Press in 2011.

Life Class

Jo Reed

Valley Press

First published in 2015 by Valley Press
Woodend, The Crescent, Scarborough, YO11 2PW
www.valleypressuk.com

First edition, first printing (March 2015)

ISBN 978-1-908853-49-3
Cat. no. VP0075

A CIP record for this book is available from the British Library.

Printed and bound in the EU by Pulsio, Paris.

www.valleypressuk.com/authors/joreed

Contents

Acknowledgements

The author would like to thank Carte Blanche of Newcastle, Helen Birmingham of Studio Gallery in Scarborough, Scarborough Flare and The Acharavi Beachbabes, for continual inspiration and support.

'Kitchen Sink Painting' was first published in A *Pocketful of Windows* (Valley Press, 2014), and appeared as a *Diamond Twig* 'poem of the month'. 'Rehearsal Room' was first published in the pamphlet *Interiors*, part of the Soho Sequence.

for my family

Asking Questions

How many times will I do the same thing?

Allow the sea to hold you,
sing your answers.

I break the waves quickly
before I've had a chance to think.

Wait in the quiet troughs,
listen to the water, watch the horizon.

Moth Life

There is a transparency
to moth life. Easy to see
how we might long to fly, but
find our nubile wings fragment
in the dust and cold
without that element
of sappy gold within our form.

We become cold, old
before our time as strings
are plucked, detached
without permission
to wind threads for others
to weave the warp and weft
of *their* belonging,
never our own.

Bus Pass Tuesdays

We sit in neat rows, at left hand side windows,
hands folded tight on clean shopping bags,
scarves tied just-so. Watching wet pavements
by shuttered shops, eyes drag each stop –
just in case we recognize a face. Metal doors
hiss and click, as the bus floor wheezes down
to kerb level *every* time. Driving in convoy
to the other side of town, we join the queue
circling roundabouts to Asda, for crumpets
and corned beef; for leaf tea, sultanas and Bero's
half pound bag of self-raising flour. We add
sardines, half a dozen eggs, a loaf of bread
to the list we've had inside our heads since
our men were taken by asbestos, coal, or war.

We smile at the security guard at the entrance,
who nods, gives a cheery combatant's grin,
sometimes a flirtatious wink, to get us inside
the colonnades for our weekly trip.
Finding the deepest trolleys, we fill our day.

Kitchen Sink Painting

I look through the kitchen door
into a scullery. I've been there before.
Time-scarred walls in a cold outhouse
where casein-painted sides blister
into sepia lines brushed through
a requisitioned cream and green existence.

I hear the *whoomph* of the gas being lit,
making steam as the stream
of hot water hits the edge
of the deep ceramic sink.
Cheaper to fill than the tin bath,
and him clean as a wink in no time.

A soft gas light glows through
from the kitchen; I taste smoke in air
warmed by clinkers from the old black range.
Using the softest of the kitchen cloths
she rubs him down,
rinses away grated soap suds.

His spindled legs are held tense
until the water warms them.
He stands firm, right hand grasping her pinny,
his left held away from his body to balance;
fist clenched, to concentrate
on the new perspective, being so high.

She finds the warmed towel, to wrap this scrap,
her little man, holds him close to her body.

Leaving

Watching the window
where sheets of rain curtain the view,
she listens to the evening traffic,
the rhythmic swish of tyres on wet roads.

Her other self glances sideways,
transfixed by the clock
pinned to the wall, dripping time;
beaded eye fixed
on the regular tremor
of the second hand,
dreaming of migration,
stars, the earth's magnetism.

Reaching underneath damp clothes,
she searches for her heart,
trying to still the flutter,
to remember which side of the rib cage
it should be beating.

A river of words have become trapped
beneath her tongue, hidden
by her mother's smile.
Leaving seems out of the question.

Needed

She was needed
to comfort him through thick and thin,
brew the tea as and when
throughout the day, then answer
the door to the Prudential,
call in at the shop for daily essentials.
At weekends get in packets of Smiths,
the Buckfast and the Barley wine
to add body to his weekend sports commentary,
the copious advice to Manchester United
and Queens Park Rangers.

Needed, to listen to wise words day after day
to pay bills as required or suffer the consequences
of an incremental overdraft, a banker's letter,
his muscular reproof.
To clean the floors and tidy up,
to wash the clothes on Mondays
and peg them on the line.

To feed his dogs, dry their feet
scrub their bowls until they shine.

Happy Families

They stand in front of the chalet,
lined up neatly at the door
according to size.
It's hard to read the emptied faces
as they were arranged, in order,
with heavy handed gestures;
told to smile on the count of three.
Posturing with the Voiglander,
trying to look the part,
he got them all in sharp focus
confined within the lens.

She stared back at the camera.

Even from this distance
you can see it in her eyes.
She couldn't remember
a world outside the frame;
negatives stacked against her
in a growing blackened pile.

Treading Water

They are centred in this rockbound place,
deep and mysterious; the forest-green surface
a sharp contrast to his winter-white back.
Pink-limbed, he holds tight
as she begins to kick towards picnic lunch,
a promised ice cream. Clinging on,
she looks to the left,
glances at the raft in the silent pool
fed from cold peat streams.

Sudden sound splashes from thrashing legs,
fracturing the surface into prisms
lit by a fickle northern sun.
His ankles, huge, distorted, angled,
as his feet, they dawdle beneath –
treading water, he keeps them both afloat,
looks down into her eyes for signs
of weakness, a faltering in her open smile.

Reggae above Ronnie's

At the top of the packing case
in tissue-paper folds, they found
the green shawl-necked dress.
Unlabelled, in a floral taffeta,
cut and stitched into a small perfection;
even darts to indicate
where breasts might fill a future space.
Tight-waisted, a flared skirt
with deepened hem in case she grew.
A dress of dresses, a Last Dance dress –
the one she never wore.

Quickstepping round Gerard Street's corner
she made a different pattern on the floor.

Norfolk Poppy

Secreted between rows of summer corn
and drab hedge shadow,
a solitary bloom gazes vacantly at the sun.
Just below, a crowd of young buds
wait to take her place, jostling for space.

At the flower heart, a pretty pod
dressed up in dark lace;
sweeps of red, silk-frilled
against the green thrill of summer,
which in the breeze send out signals:
'Stop. Stop here.'

Ripening to the sound of bees,
dizzy in the heat, working against time,
she takes on all comers.
Finally, no pretence, the hard truth,
the seed sets, held tight
on a strong deflowered stem.

The Rehearsal Room

She climbs the stairs
to the rehearsal room,
breathes in the distilled spores
of scores of other dancers
who have practised at this barre before,
bandaged their feet sat on the floor.

She tries to forget the hot stale smell
of crowded platforms, the constant stares
of emboldened men that she ignores.
Sipping lukewarm coffee from the flask,
she settles to the task of warming
muscles against unpolished boards,
willing her tired legs back and forth.

A crocodile of tourists descends
from a coach, winds its way
through narrow streets, cameras poised
to capture Soho's thrilling secrets; lens
upturned at a disturbance of pigeons.
They try to locate the noise –
a raucous song by Shirley Bassey –
see only a slim hand
resting on an open windowsill.

The place seems colder. Chilled air
sets off gooseflesh on her bare arms.
She stands, gazes her fill at the face
in the mirror, drops her shoulders,
lifts her arms and poised, bends plie;
begins the hard daily grind
behind the decorative facade,
tries to remember if she took the pill.

Dirty Linen

The Banshy boys danced foxtrot
on Saturday nights with unpolished girls
who, seen and not heard,
didn't put a word out of place
between hanging green bottles
or sweet Sunday hedgerow.
Too late by Monday to fold a message,
put a stopper to it.

They stood each day in charitable waters,
scrubbing collar and cuff,
keeping the army on its toes,
looking for links in the steam,
between the Lord's flowing goodness
and the cleansing carbolic stream;
ironing out the meanings of love,
the loss of a child, mangled womanhood.

Brancaster Beach 1949

Children of the flat earth society
pose by a cold east-coast lagoon,
fringed with distant muddy waves
that slowly inch toward the dunes.

They stare into the camera's eye
each with a different *mein*, all smile,
wondering, as they each comply,
about the lie of land so near the sea.

They sail, completely chartless,
across a wealth of wind-ribbed sand
with furrows of sharp marram grass
toward an indistinct horizon.

They find globular flints, split apart;
their fine-grained white casing
masking magma-black hearts,
hidden arrowhead and axe blade,

that leave sharp warning messages
between long green laver bands,
strewn along stone-scattered passages
of spring pale, wind-whipped strand.

Small toes scratch bare alphabets
carefully traced in the damp shore,
their rune casting, declarations,
gently erased by the afternoon tide.

Panther

He straddled the huge bike,
smiling at the camera, the dog
balanced on the rear,
grinning like Chaplin in fear.
He collected cable and carburettor
from enthusiasts gone cold
through conscription,
lack of work or dole.

Frame and chassis, hidden
tank and clutch he found
in sheds, cobbled alleyways
and illegal city middens;
he hand-built the beast in a back yard,
adding the engine at a time
when he could only just touch
his boots to the ground.

The once-rough engine purred
when he raced heavy lorries
along the Great North Road.
Too heavy to handle
as it roared past Scotch Corner,
it pounced on a hedge, turned,
bit him in the face.
The old army surgeon
wearied by thoughts of war
stitched cheek and chin neatly into place;
said the scar would make him look tough
for what was in store.

Off Yarmouth

Granddad died off Yarmouth.
The last to leave the boat we're told,
after defending the Thames
from the enemy below
in the last year of the war.

Blown out of the water,
remains never found,
his name is carved on a cenotaph
in bold Roman letters somewhere
along the new river path.

Such a small remembrance.

My grandma said she found it hard
to cope, to remember his face,
after he had drowned; she
married a miner after the war,
knowing he'd stay earthbound.

Joining the Dots

He worked in wood, joining dusty corners of the poet's life.
They were first-name friends on weekends
as George escaped home, earned extra;
Philip made manly small talk, away from books and women.

Christmas Present

Just before Christmas it was decided
that they would have healthy lives;
exercise, become family fit.
He got the silver dream-racer,
with the elegantly narrow seat
dropped handle bars,
and lightweight wheels;
the boys rode mountain bikes
all sturdy and bright in primary colours.

She watched through the window
overlooking the road
at their delight as they turned right
for the estuarine shore –
tried to fix the brake
on the exercise bike
bolted tightly to the floor.

Day Trips

There are day trips to bus stations
behind shabby Esplanades,
where the pakamac brigade
loose fusillades of cardboard cups
as they scrat about in half-closed Shoppes;
express admiration
for each other's bargain buys
in Victorian shelters and amusement arcades.

It's a slow parting,
far beyond thoughts of nip and tuck;
saving face, just in case there is another way
to share the pain of leaving.
Hips click a relentless morse code
as assorted matrons' shortened shopping lists
to suit the pocket – the low cholesterol diet –
reflect a quiet sort of supper,
a despair of supermarket dinners,
just for one.

Wired

A metal wire inserted in a vein
reaches branches beyond,
touches on dark secrets, ancient tales
of *amglyda*, the unknown land.
She hears needles clicking
sharp time with the melody
of a bellowing beast outside the door;
notes the smell of rain
on sun-warmed floors
before it seeps
into a single strand, thinner than
the lifeline disappearing
in the palm of her left hand.

Marginal

Stilled at the edge,
where shallow pools back and fill
according to phases of the moon,

the Humbolt current, solar wind;
movements not of my making.
Here I am still sea – without chart

sextant or ship, with days
when equinoxal swells
begin to overwhelm the space

I have chosen; the estuarial flow,
the shallow end,
filtering through limpet and barnacle

to kiss the sedge; the fingertips
of land, a pool of quiet
right here, in the margin.

Japanese Print

The horses turn their backs
against linear rain.
The men complain,
capes wet
beneath woven hats.

Women, fashioned
and patterned into
a passion of obscurity,
become woven into
a tea garden's pleasure.

Wings of gray lace
powder the face of the moon,
brush the cheek
to reach the reflection
in his eyes –
burn in her cold glance.

Tasting the Sea

You can feel it way up here
where the fret is hung on spider webs,
collects in lichen on old stone steps.
Opaque fog saturates, reaches
between the rushy edges of the mere,
mists and beads each hair
on our bare arms. Up here,
where air is soft and wet on the skin,
we taste it on our lips, speech
dries upon our salted tongues.
We walk down to where there is a hush,
a whisper, of a veiled and silent sea.

Turtle Song

Beneath the surface
a turtle sings, fathoms deep,
a boy held safe upon her back.

Moving House in November

Another shift, a sideways lurch
as chestnuts split their carapace,
reveal a soft smooth emptiness,
white against darkening drifts
of blunt five-fingered leaves.
Boys discard these outer parts,
speckled, spikey, hardened, green,
for the bronzed surfaced weaponry
of a conqueror's campaign dreams.
I pile them on painted wicker chairs,
a broken blanket box; old familiars,
waiting for me to throw the torch.

Lighting a Candle in Corfu

Here, the church below my sister's home
awaits spring and Clean Monday,
chairs stacked untidily along each wall.
In stale warm air, I cross the wooden floor,
stirring winter dust into low clouds
powdered with sunlight from the open door,
and light a slender candle for my daughter,
the thirty years that I could never know.

Beyond St. Niki's icons on the wall
I touch the face of Madonna With Child;
overlaid in a gilded case, the glow
separates them from my reality. Tears fall.

The cat has followed us, rumbustious,
doubling his size, fluffing up his fur,
remembering the few days he became
locked in – a 'Keeper of the Faith' by mistake,
still wanting to make his mark.
Captured and cradled in my sister's arms,
he purrs the prayer that I can't sound
through clotted throat.
He precedes us as we leave,
beating the boundary twice,
tail ramrod-high, devoted
master of this small ceremony.

Convalescence

A son had made a curving shore
with shingle waves and stony foam
breaking against the old foundations,
where a storm-blown greenhouse
had been anchored long before.

Looking through Victorian glass
at the faded painting, she saw sunlight
filtering through orchids, imagined
the sweet delight of pineapple in winter,
out of season, glowing in the twilight.

The smell of orange blossom grew
as ghost willows whitened and froze
in winter fogs; cold comfort mists
rose round rusting containers, covered
with shanties, and bedraggled crows.

Pillowed deep in bleached canvas
she dozed on the summer beach,
listened to the sound of vast seas
billowing through the poplar trees,
discovered her land legs once more.

In the Drawing Room

Today I am a pirate ship;
fat feather cushions set sail for Africay,
embroidered rafts to leap upon
and cross the heavy sea between
here and the bay window
where they've taken
round brass trays of another age,
burnished them into Viking shields
to hang along a soft top deck
of old loose covers, hand sewn
in William Morris green,
placed to reflect the afternoon sun
into the enemy eyes when they come
to glare through the window at dusk,
when brigands walk the plank
heading for a kitchen tea.

Yesterday I was a sick bed
as they fussed over one of them,
and his dog – who peed
all over my ornately-carved feet in sympathy.
Tonight I will dream of the days
before they came, when I was flanked
by high-backed chairs
made for the tall men of the family,
now outranked by a Pirate Queen.

Wood and Water

The printer's relationship
with paper is easy;
she cuts it back,
gives it more room.

Folding the paper,
admiring its curve,
she strokes it into place;
an image appears.

Leaning forward, she
adds cadmium red
to the block with
a short-handled brush.
Stands back,
satisfied with its depth.

Mixes more red,
then black –
advances them with green.

The air is drying the paint.
A window is closed,
the wind sighs.

Horsehair, soft and springy,
takes up the pigment,
lets it flow from the tip.

Dampened, Kozo paper
pressed down on the block
absorbs all its colour.

Now the black,
linear, geometric,
frames the spiral.
We want to touch.

Skirling, the buren sounds
gentle against the surface;
pulls back, done.

Cellular forms
appear on paper,
a small magic
held in the fibres.

They contain
the updraught,
huge raindrops fall
from deep inside
a cloud formation,
flood the city –
a pumpkin storm.

From the sharp cut
of a steel blade
in hardwood handle,
water flows.

How to Climb a Tower

Step upward one tread at a time,
feel the wood give beneath your feet.
Move upward toward the light.
Watch the way others cling to the rail
and like them, lean inward away from the edge.
Determine not to look down.
Feel your knuckles tighten,
see them whiten the higher you go.
(Don't wait for me I'm fine, I'll be okay when I get there.)

At the top, stand stone-still,
become your own cairn,
will your breath into a circle,
the confined space of a paper bag
until your heart slows to its usual pace.
Become a conjuror without assistant –
make a doubloon skate into plaice,
eggs appear from coiled air
behind the ringmaster's ear.
Finally, when brave enough to descend
make ridiculous excuses for the late arrival,
continue writing small
on bleached blue *par avion* paper.

Freud's Consulting Room Cushion

Hand-woven in Afghanistan
with finest silks in ancient pattern;
gifted, I became magical,
flew around the world
at my master's feet –
all the way back to Ethiopia.

Diplomats, Warlords, even Kings
made obeisance to me;
the only one invited
to all the Great Ceremonies.
Even the Assassination,
though it was a quiet occasion that time.

Now, I listen to sad secrets,
fearful dreams and imagined slights,
pillow hysterical hair;
but always here, in this grey place.
Never there, with him,
in the sunlit Halls of Paradise.

Upholstery

Delivered dirty from the auction,
it had lived through many lives before.
Wall-hung for safekeeping, small and squat,
spare and square, the barley twist legs braced
in dusty space, held on through winter's waste
covered in mould and spiders lace, until...

> She bought herringbone webbing,
> a hickory hammer, rough woven hessian,
> calico, cream linen and fine waxed twine.

Next spring, worn leather was ripped, and stripped
back to bonewood, its skeletal frame renewed –
freed to breathe in the space allowed
by such a basic disassembling. The same chair
was disjointed, cleaned, each limb secured
with a carpenter's care, some good wood glue.

> She tacked on herringbone webbing
> with her hickory hammer, rough woven hessian,
> calico, cream linen and fine waxed twine.

The chair travels through the seasons –
overwinters in dark corners, brightens each space
with Thracian gold; migrates each summer
to the hall, welcomes sunhats, plastic buckets,
and sandy beach balls. This spring, in the bedroom,
the chair sits between wardrobe and Easter, holds
the 'maybe' collection for travel abroad.

The New Dress

In this dress I will abseil down Everest,
tread my tightrope with a new dexterity
above the Tyne, spin on a pin with angels
amazed in the nave of Beverley Minster.

In this dress I'll dance down red carpets
without leaving marks, face down the dog
barking black through night's blanket,
then pillow my head in unbroken sleep.

In this dress, with promises I can keep,
I'll lob secret messages all over the net,
deal daily with Talk Talk, and other things
sinister, eat caviar for breakfast, place bets

on that missing Minister of State, wassail
with a choir on the deck of Invincible
as she flags sad goodbyes, ship to shore;
eat oysters on Fridays, *always* ask for more.

I will finish poems, win prizes galore,
ignore the front cover of *Grazia*, where
they have a portrait of me – in *this dress* –
holding the Oscar for 'Best Screenplay'.

In this dress, I'll buy an old printing press,
wing-walk my Cessna on the way to Venice,
eat fritto misto overlooking the sea,
bombard men with trifle whenever I please.

The Engineers

for the Shackells of Quince Cottage

A quiet night at the bar saw him
drinking halves, biding time, until
the ladies who lunch sailed in;
late, en masse, a melee intent
on fun in Felsham that night, who
took command of the round table
in the bay of the Six Bells –
clever engineers, all of them.

He, dapper in cords and navy crew,
smiled, said he couldn't remember
what she wore, though admired
her pretty sandals; the height
of gallantry that night. Friends
watched in delight as their talk grew;
of art school, bohemian heydays –
all the ways they already knew
each other, named London streets
where, unknowing, they had passed
each week, though on the other side.

Two trees rooted in the same past,
parched of artesian waters, took in
Suffolk rain, sprung bud and leaf
along the route of their footprints
to every Cafe Rouge in France and Spain;
until now, when they feast with you
on Aphrodite's fruit, the golden Quince.

Stuffed Shirts

Cellophane-wrapped shirts slide free,
parade in good order down Valley Road,
always dressing to the left, but
told never to swim alone in cut-glass seas;
they whirl round lamp posts like stags in rut.

Unwrapped, they become bold;
flap lazily on the breeze, unfurl,
cuff passing herring gulls, fold
flat sleeves round hen's angels, those
lost girls skirling towards matrimony;

twirl out to sea, in a mastery of navigation unknown
in the cutting rooms of St. James.
Soaring over donkeys lined up on cold sands,
they plummet down in formation,
encourage stampede, until, full of wind

they begin to tire, link sleeves, spin
round the harbour at a slower rate of knots.
Unbuttoned eyelets look down in a row,
spy clean sheets on backyard washing lines,
neatly peg themselves into a new plot.

February

It was always an awkward month, February.
Not the newness of the year any more,
Valentine's day slap-bang in the middle;
without Prince Charming, of course,
he died years ago. She sat knitting,
watching *Emmerdale* or *EastEnders*,
anything really, as long as there was *talk*
and lots of it; something she'd missed
out on before, when winding her wool
from old skeins into neat balls.
Never one for words, was Walter.
Taciturn and *Morose* the dictionary said.

'Miserable old git,' joked Enid to Grace
in the village hall, still missing him,
looking for the latest knitting pattern,
the one for the Oxfam Easter rabbit.

She would sew a smile on its face,
beneath the moustache,
put him in the carrier bag with the others.

Young Mermaid

She eats ocean eggs from silver mussel shells,
sand-sugared, spoons in the yellow coral cake
found drifting in the distant roar of shingle.
Listening to the sharp bark of an excited dog
pacing back and forth on ridged wet sand,
seeking, she begins scraping delicate weed
east toward the raised wings of sandbars.
Hiding herself in the dunes
she listens to the roar of jets overhead
trailing exhaustion past marker posts
like dead men's fingers pointing landwards.
Peach-coloured seaweed strands
wrap around an old tyre
like discarded underwear.
Poking a jellyfish with a bleached stick,
she watches it shiver at gravity,
its upper parts transparent,
the lower marked like a turtle
stranded by the sea an hour or so ago.
She begins the search for gold
near the last line of flat skimming stones,
dips dry fins in the water pools beneath.

Instructions

Make a shroud of linen thread,
weave violets into the weft
of all those years; wrap me neat
with hands on heart,
to keep the love I hold for you
within my bed of green plait willow,
a silken pillow
beneath my feet.

A View of Ithaka

It's there,
in that measured square
on the horizon. Only a few more
broken lines on the map.
I had seen it from Zakinthos
years ago, but didn't know
the look of it
or recognise its worth
across that flow of Ionian sea;

never realised how close
it had become until that rainy
afternoon when I let go of the tiller,
drank deep of Harry's wine,
then examined the chart
inside its circled purple stain.

Here, I sit on limestone sills
below St. Spiridon's and
the Monastery, listen to the slow
beat of my heart,
note the current that takes
the ferries past your shore
toward the canal,
begin to plan the next voyage.

Cartography

This line is for the first born, a practicing pirate,
this one for a child of less than a year,
this one a lifeline disguised as a burglar,
this one
the split stone, the veering,
a longitude of late birthing,
the route on my map
that led me to here.